SPOTLIGHT ON EXPLORERS AND COLONIZATION™

PEDRO ÁLVARES CABRAL

First European Explorer of Brazil

ANN BYERS

ROSEN
PUBLISHING®

New York

Published in 2017 by The Rosen Publishing Group, Inc.
29 East 21st Street, New York, NY 10010

First Edition

Library of Congress Cataloging-in-Publication Data

Names: Byers, Ann, author.
Title: Pedro Álvares Cabral : first European explorer of Brazil / Ann Byers.
Description: First edition. | New York : Rosen Publishing, [2017] | Series:
Spotlight on explorers and colonization | Includes bibliographical
references and index.
Identifiers: LCCN 2016001008| ISBN 9781477788233 (library bound) | ISBN
9781477788219 (pbk.) | ISBN 9781477788226 (6-pack)
Subjects: LCSH: Cabral, Pedro Alvares, -1520?--Juvenile literature. |
Brazil--Discovery and exploration--Portuguese--Juvenile literature. |
Portugal--History--Period of discoveries, 1385-1580--Juvenile literature.
| Explorers--Portugal--History--Juvenile literature. |
Explorers--Brazil--History--Juvenile literature.
Classification: LCC E125.C11 B95 2016 | DDC 910.92/2--dc23
LC record available at http://lccn.loc.gov/2016001008

Manufactured in the United States of America

CONTENTS

AGE OF EXPLORATION

In the fourteenth century (1300–1399), people in Europe knew little about the world around them. They knew India was far to the east and Africa was across the Mediterranean Sea. Merchants brought spices, silk cloth, and other items to Europe from Asia. Traders brought gold and ivory from Africa. Europeans also wanted products from India, especially the spices. At this time, however, the Italians controlled the trade with India, and they charged high prices.

People who lived in what is now Turkey—Ottomans, whom the Europeans called Arabs—began spreading into eastern Europe and North Africa. In 1453, they

Europeans used spices to flavor and color their foods. They also thought some spices helped digestion and combatted fevers, headaches, and bad breath.

captured the cities on the Mediterranean that led to the trade routes and blocked them.

So Europeans decided to try to get to India a different way, by sailing south on the Atlantic Ocean. This was the beginning of the Age of Exploration, also called the Age of Discovery.

PORTUGAL VS. SPAIN

Portugal was the first country to explore new trade routes, followed by Spain. Christopher Columbus, an Italian living in Portugal, thought he could reach India by sailing west across the Atlantic Ocean. But Portugal's king believed the best way to India was to go south, around Africa. Portugal would not pay for Columbus's expedition, but Spain did. When Columbus discovered a New World by landing in the Caribbean, both Spain and Portugal wanted it. European rulers thought they could claim and take over any country that did not have a Christian ruler.

This 1502 map shows the little that was known of Brazil (with the three parrots) east of the Line of Demarcation. The land north of Brazil, marked "Territory of the King of Portugal," is Newfoundland.

The two countries let the Pope settle their argument. The Pope drew a line on a map, dividing the world in half. Spain could have all new land west of the line, and Portugal could claim any new territory east of the line. The countries agreed by signing the Treaty of Tordesillas. The Portuguese were happy with the treaty because it gave them land in Africa and Asia.

AROUND AFRICA TO INDIA

Portugal began its sea-going exploration around 1415 under Prince Henry the Navigator. At first, the Portuguese sailors just explored the west coast of Africa. They developed new kinds of ships and made maps of the lands they found. Before long, they also wanted to find a way around Africa to India. No one knew how big Africa was. In 1488, Bartolomeu Dias reached the southernmost point of the continent. Portugal's king named it Cape of Good Hope because its discovery gave him hope of getting to India by sailing around Africa.

Ten years later, Vasco da Gama sailed around the cape and made it all the way to Calicut, India. He asked Calicut's ruler to let

Vasco da Gama encourages his men during a storm at the Cape of Good Hope in this modern illustration. Three of four ships and 54 of 170 men survived the two-year (1497–1498) trip.

him put a Portuguese trading station in the city. But the ruler was unhappy with the cheap gifts da Gama offered, and he already had agreements with Arab traders. Da Gama went back to Portugal without a trade deal, but he had found the sea route to India.

PEDRO CABRAL, CAPTAIN

Vasco da Gama returned to Portugal in 1499. King Manuel I decided to send a second expedition to try again to set up a trading center in India. The man he put in charge of the voyage was Pedro Álvares Cabral.

Cabral was born in 1467 to a noble family. His father was lord of the Castle of Belmonte, and his mother was a descendant of the first king of Portugal. Because he was a noble, Pedro received a good education in math, science, and other subjects. The king made Cabral one of his counselors and appointed him a knight of the military Order of Christ.

Built as a fort in 1266, Belmonte Castle was given to the Cabral family by King Alfonso V in 1446. Pedro Cabral was born here. Today the castle is a national monument.

There is no record that Cabral, who was thirty-three years old in 1500, had ever been a soldier or sailor. Noblemen were often given jobs as leaders whether they had experience or not. Cabral just had to find good sailors to lead his expedition halfway around the world.

CABRAL PREPARES

King Manuel gave Cabral several tasks to accomplish. The most important was to do what da Gama had failed to do: get the ruler of Calicut, India, to let Portugal put a factory—a trade center—in his city. He was also supposed to buy spices and bring them home with him.

Another task was to find Sofala, a port in East Africa. Many years earlier, an explorer traveling over land had discovered the port where African merchants brought their gold. The king wanted Cabral to find Sofala again and put a factory there. The last task was to take missionaries to India to spread Christianity there.

A MARKET SCENE AT SOFALA IN 1505.

This drawing of a 1505 market in Sofala, Mozambique, shows women selling fruits and spices. Sofala was best known among traders for ivory and gold brought from the interior of Africa.

Cabral got thirteen ships ready for the journey. He found captains and 1,500 men willing to go with him. He loaded the ships with expensive gifts for the ruler of Calicut, goods to trade for spices, and supplies. On March 9, 1500, he was ready.

ON THE ATLANTIC

To get to India, Cabral followed the route da Gama had taken three years earlier. Da Gama had figured out how to sail with the ocean currents instead of against them. Rather than heading straight down the coast of Africa, his course took Cabral in a wide arc around the continent.

After almost a week at sea, the fleet reached the Cape Verde Islands. One ship was missing, probably sunk, and Cabral had to sail on without it. Instead of going directly south, he went southwest, away from Africa. His plan was to ride the ocean currents until he crossed the equator. Far south of the

Cabral called this landing spot "Porto Seguro," meaning "Safe Port." He is pictured here onshore with soldiers who carry the banner of his military order. Curious natives watch the landing party.

equator, the currents and the winds would carry the ships southeast, past the Cape of Good Hope.

In making the arc, Cabral swung farther west than da Gama had gone. On April 22, Cabral's men spotted a mountain, flat land, and trees. They had come to what would become the country of Brazil.

ASHORE

When the fleet landed in Brazil, Cabral sent Captain Nicolau Coelho ashore in a small boat. About twenty natives ran toward Coelho. They had bows and arrows, but they were not holding them in a threatening way. Coelho motioned for them to put their weapons down, and they did. To show he was friendly, the captain offered gifts; he threw three hats to the natives. The men accepted the gifts and offered presents to Coelho in return: a headdress of parrot feathers and a string of beads.

The natives belonged to one of the Tupí tribes. The tribes sometimes fought one another, but the people were friendly to the visitors. They had no reason to hurt them or

The Asurini do Tocantins are Tupí people, one of 240 native tribes that live in Brazil today. They paint their bodies and wear colorful headdresses, much like the Brazilians Cabral met, and they hunt and fish.

be afraid of them. Cabral brought two curious natives on his ship. He offered them food and drink, which they spat out. The two natives were comfortable enough with the Portuguese to sleep on the boat.

The next day Cabral ordered four of his men to mix with the natives. The men were *degredados*, criminals. Instead of going to prison, their punishment was to go with the explorers to do dangerous tasks no one else would do. If the natives turned out to be savage, the criminals would be hurt, not the explorers.

Fortunately, the natives were not hostile. They took the degredados inland about three miles (five kilometers) to their little village. They gave them roots and seeds to eat. The men gave the natives some small trinkets in exchange for parrots, monkeys, and cloth made of feathers. The men spent the day in the village, but at night the Tupís made them leave.

Cabral explored several miles of the coast. He did not find gold, silver, iron, or anything else of great value. What he did find was a new world that would become a significant part of a Portuguese empire that would last five hundred years.

Cabral first came ashore in Brazil near a small mountain he called "Monte Pascoal," or "Easter Mount." Two days later he traveled north to Porto Seguro, where he claimed the land for Portugal.

CLAIMING BRAZIL

Cabral stayed in Brazil for only ten days. He had an assignment to accomplish on the other side of the Atlantic. But he had one more piece of business in America. He had landed on a part of South America that bulged out just slightly east of the Treaty of Tordesillas line. That meant the new land belonged to Portugal. But with Spain also exploring in the Americas, he had to make sure Spain would not try to claim this territory.

Cabral's men set up a large cross with the official symbol of the king of Portugal on it. It stood as a monument, announcing that Brazil belonged to Portugal. Cabral then sent one of his ships back to Portugal with the news of his discovery.

After a priest held a religious service, Cabral claimed the "Island of the True Cross," as he named Brazil, for Portugal. The banner he holds has the emblem of his military order, the Order of Christ.

To make extra sure no other country would take Brazil from Portugal, Cabral left two of the degregados there. Their job was to learn more about the land and the natives. Soon Portugal would send settlers.

DISCOVERY: ACCIDENT OR PLANNED?

Brazilians celebrate Cabral as the man who discovered their country. But Cabral was not the first European to see Brazil. Three months before Cabral's voyage, the Spaniard Vicente Yáñez Pinzón landed on the coast of Brazil. Months before that, the Italian Amerigo Vespucci, sailing for Spain, may have explored some of northern Brazil. Other Spanish adventurers also visited parts of South America.

Many people believe Cabral was blown off course and came to Brazil by accident. Others think he "stumbled on" South America on purpose. Portugal's King Manuel

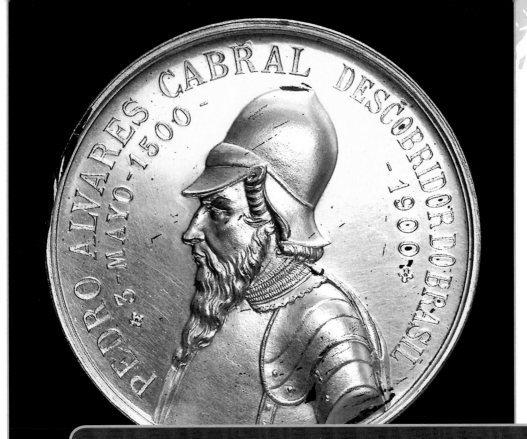

Cabral's discovery of Brazil is celebrated on April 22. Both Brazil and Portugal have issued postage stamps commemorating the event. On this medal marking four hundred years since the discovery, Cabral is pictured in military armor.

may have suspected there was unclaimed land east of the Treaty of Tordesillas line. Portuguese sailors had been exploring the Atlantic for years, and at least one of them had reported spotting a large landmass. Some people think the king told Cabral to look for that land and claim it before Spain tried to beat them to it. No one really knows.

TO AFRICA

When Cabral left Brazil, he turned east, toward the southern tip of Africa. Sailing was smooth until the fleet got close to the Cape of Good Hope, where storms battered the ships. For six days, the crews struggled against the wind and waves. Four ships sank with everyone on board. One was the boat captained by Bartolomeu Dias, the first European to sail this far south. He had named the spot the Cape of Storms.

Cabral made it through the storm to the island of Mozambique. Five other captains also reached the island. Only Diogo Dias, Bartolomeu's brother, was missing. The Dias brothers were not supposed to go all the way to India; their assignment was to set up a factory in the African gold port of Sofala.

Bartolomeu Dias (1450–1500) sailed on three famous voyages. He was the first European to reach Africa's southern tip, he sailed partway with Vasco da Gama, and he was with Cabral in Brazil.

Cabral assumed Dias was already searching for Sofala, so he didn't wait for him. He loaded the six ships with fresh supplies and set out again.

EAST AFRICA

Following da Gama's route, Cabral stopped at African ports both to refresh his supplies and to trade. He bypassed Mombasa because the people there had been unfriendly to da Gama. Instead, he went to Kilwa. He knew from earlier overland explorers that Kilwa was a large trading center. He tried to negotiate a treaty with the person in charge, but he was not successful. He continued north, to Malindi, which had treated da Gama well.

He could not remain long in Africa because the sailors had to catch the summer monsoon winds to India. If they waited too long, the winter winds could be as disastrous as the storms at the cape had been. He hired two pilots who could guide him the rest of the way. He left two degredados in Malindi to maintain positive relations and trade between Portugal and East Africa. Then he headed east across the Indian Ocean.

In 1505 the Portuguese forced their rule on Kilwa and built this fort to protect their trading interests there. They did not rule well. Within a few years, Kilwa sank into chaos, and the Portuguese left.

"CITY OF SPICES"

On September 13, 1500, Cabral finally reached his destination: Calicut, India. Before meeting with the zamorin, the ruler of Calicut, the two parties exchanged hostages because they didn't trust each other. Cabral took Indians onto his ships, while the Indians held some of his men. Careful not to repeat da Gama's mistake, Cabral presented the zamorin with rich gifts.

This zamorin was not the same one who had been angry with da Gama; that one had died. The new zamorin was pleased with Cabral and his gifts. He agreed to a treaty and told Cabral he could set up a trade factory in his city.

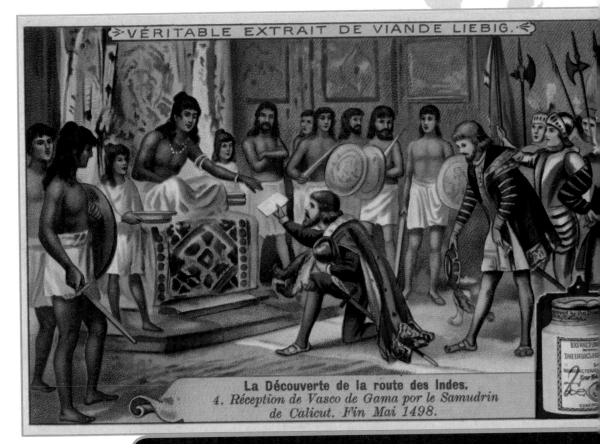

La Découverte de la route des Indes.
4. Réception de Vasco de Gama por le Samudrin de Calicut. Fin Mai 1498.

Two years before Cabral came to India, Vasco da Gama presented the Zamorin of Calicut with a letter of friendship from the king of Portugal. The Zamorin's uneasy guards stand with drawn swords.

The man Cabral had brought to be the Calicut factor went ashore with about seventy men and began building the factory. Cabral had successfully completed his mission. Now all he had to do was wait for the factor to purchase enough spices to load up his ships. Then he could go home.

DEADLY COMPETITION

In two months in Calicut, only two of Cabral's six ships were filled with the spices they had come to get. The problem was the Arab merchants. For many years, they had held a monopoly; they were the only traders who bought goods in India and sold them in Europe. They did everything they could to keep the Portuguese factor from obtaining materials Portugal would sell in Europe.

Cabral complained to the zamorin, but the ruler did nothing. Frustrated, Cabral seized an Arab ship that was in the harbor and took its cargo, claiming it should be his. The Arabs, in turn, started a riot on shore. They

An illustration from the fifteenth-century book *The Travels of Marco Polo*, originally written in 1298, shows Western and Eastern traders exchanging spices, cloth, and other goods at a trading post in Asia.

blocked Cabral's ships from coming close enough for anyone to get off. Cabral watched helplessly as a mob attacked the Portuguese factory. After three hours, more than fifty Portuguese were dead. A few escaped by jumping into the water and swimming to the ships.

REVENGE

The massacre of his men in Calicut outraged Cabral. Not only had he lost people, but he had also lost money. All the goods he brought for trading were in the destroyed factory, and he could not get them back. He would return to Portugal with very few spices.

In anger and to make up for his losses, Cabral ordered his men to capture ten boats belonging to Arab merchants. They killed all the Arabs on board and transferred the cargo to their own vessels. Then they set fire to the empty merchant ships.

Cabral was also angry with the zamorin. The Indian ruler had not tried to stop the massacre. In fact, some of the zamorin's

The artillery of Cabral's ships overwhelmed the city of Calicut and the ships in its harbor. The typical Portuguese caravel carried four heavy cannons, six lighter cannons, and ten or twelve smaller guns.

guards were part of the riot. So as the fleet left, Cabral told his crew to aim their ships' guns toward the shore. For one full day, cannonballs rained down on Calicut, killing hundreds.

COCHIN

The trade agreement with Calicut was gone, and Cabral had very few spices to take back to the king. He had to find another trading center and make a deal there. Luckily, there were other cities along the Malabar coast of India. Cabral sailed south to the port of Cochin.

Cochin and Calicut were rivals. They wanted to do business with the same merchants, but Calicut usually won. In order to trade, the raja (ruler) of Cochin had to pay a fee to Calicut's zamorin. So when the raja heard the Portuguese fleet had nearly destroyed Calicut, he welcomed Cabral eagerly.

Negotiating a treaty was easy. The raja wanted to defeat Calicut, so Cabral promised that Portugal would help him. In return, the raja allowed a Portuguese factory to be built in his city and protected it from the Arabs. Cabral loaded his ships with Cochin's spices and went home.

With the raja's permission, Portugal built a fort on the waterfront of Cochin in 1503, named after Portugal's King Manuel. The fort was the beginning of Portuguese control of India.

HOMEWARD BOUND

On July 21, 1501, sixteen months after beginning the expedition, Cabral landed in Portugal. Counting the boat that had been sent home from Brazil, seven of the original thirteen ships had survived the journey. But only five brought back treasures from India.

Cabral's report was disappointing. He had lost half his men, including the famous Bartolomeu Dias. There was no factory at Calicut; in fact, Calicut would not welcome any new expedition from Portugal. No one had visited the African gold port of Sofala. The missionaries had not converted anyone to Christianity.

In the sixteenth century, many merchants doing business in Europe lived in Portuguese colonies along the coasts of India. Here a Portuguese merchant is welcomed by his wife and their Indian servants.

But there was some good news. The spices were fewer than expected, but they would sell well in Europe. Although Calicut was lost, there was a factory in the smaller city of Cochin. And Portugal had land in the Americas. If nothing more, Brazil would at least be a stopping place for more trips to India.

NO MORE EXPEDITIONS

When Cabral returned to Portugal, King Manuel planned another mission to India. Should he send Cabral again? Some of the king's advisors said no. Cabral had lost six ships and many men, and he had ruined all hope of trade with Calicut. He had failed in every task assigned him.

Should the king send Vasco da Gama, who had discovered the sea route to India? Some advisors wanted da Gama in charge of the expedition. The king offered the job to Cabral first but later decided on da Gama instead.

Historians are not sure exactly what happened. Some think Cabral turned the

Under King Manuel I (1469–1521), Portugal rose from a tiny country to a wealthy global empire. Manuel the Fortunate, as he was later known, sent Vasco da Gama and Cabral on their voyages, dominated the trade routes, and colonized Africa and India.

mission down because he would have to share command with da Gama's uncle. Others believe the king did not trust Cabral's ability and purposely made an offer Cabral would not accept. Whatever the reason, Cabral did not go on any more expeditions. He left the king's service and faded into history.

A PLACE IN HISTORY

For many years, Cabral's achievements were lost in the shadow of more famous explorers. But his voyage shaped world history. Though da Gama found the route to India, Cabral was the one who established trade there. Cabral broke the monopoly of the Arab merchants. Other European countries raced to find trading partners in India. Spanish, French, Dutch, and British ships began sailing the Atlantic. Their trading trips led them to new lands, and colonies sprang up all over Africa, the East Indies, and the Americas.

The factory Cabral started in Cochin, the first Portuguese one in India, grew into a fort.

In this statue of Cabral in Belmonte, Portugal, the explorer holds an astrolabe, a navigational instrument; a sword, because he belonged to a military order; and a cross, because he claimed to sail in service to his faith.

From there, Portugal started colonies along the coasts of Africa, India, and the islands east of India. Portugal's head start in the spice trade enabled it to build the largest and longest lasting empire of any European nation. Because of Cabral, that empire included Brazil, where Portuguese is still the official language.

GLOSSARY

arc A line that is part of a circle.

cargo Materials carried on a truck, train, ship, or airplane.

current The flow of water in a certain direction.

degredado In Portugal, a convicted criminal who was punished by being forced to leave the country and perform difficult and dangerous tasks.

descendant Child, niece, or nephew of a person; grandchild; great niece or nephew; great grandchild; great-great niece or nephew; etc.

expedition A trip that has a specific purpose.

factory A place where business is conducted.

fleet A group of ships.

headdress A covering for the head, usually bigger and decorated more than a hat.

hostage A person held by one party in order to force another party to do something.

massacre The killing of many people, often people who are helpless to defend themselves.

monopoly The only one with control of, or right to something.

navigator A person who decides what course to travel.

Ottoman A Turkish person who was part of the Ottoman Empire.

raja The title for a prince or chief among some peoples of India.

zamorin The title of the ruler of Calicut, India.

Instituto Socioambiental
São Paulo Av., Higienópolis
901 SL 30
São Paulo 01238-001
Brazil
Website: http://pib.socioambiental.org/en
The Instituto Socioambiental provides information and
advocates for the indigenous people (natives) of
Brazil. The website has information on their history
and present conditions.

Mariners' Museum
100 Museum Drive
Newport News, VA 23606
(757) 596-2222
Website: http://www.marinersmuseum.org
The Mariners' Museum houses objects, displays,
and exhibitions about the history of sea-going
activities. The materials are from ancient times to
the present day and from all over the world.

National Historical Museum of Brazil (Museu Histórico
Nacional)
Praça Marechal Âncora, Próximo à Praça XV
20.21-200 – Centro
Rio de Janeiro, RJ
Brazil

(55 21) 32990300 - 32990324
Website: http://www.museuhistoriconacional.com.br
   /ingles
Originally built as a fort in 1603, the National Historical
   Museum of Brazil has many items from Portugal
   as well as Brazil, showing Brazil's history through
   many permanent and traveling exhibitions.

National Museum of Brazil
Quinta da Boa Vista
São Cristóvão
Rio de Janeiro, RJ, 20940-040
Brazil
(55 21) 3938-6900
Website: http://www.museunacional.ufrj.br
Established for scientific research in 1818 by
   Portuguese King João VI, the museum houses
   examples of plants and animals of Brazil as well as
   items from the country's early history, including from
   natives.

Websites

Because of the changing nature of Internet links,
Rosen Publishing has developed an online list of
websites related to the subject of this book. This site is
updated regularly. Please use this link to access this list:

http://www.rosenlinks.com/SEC/cabral

Aronson, Marc, and John W. Glenn. *The World Made New: Why the Age of Exploration Happened and How It Changed the World.* Washington, DC: National Geographic, 2007.

Ceceri, Kathryn. *The Silk Road: 20 Projects Explore the World's Most Famous Trade Route.* White River Junction, VT: Nomad Press, 2011.

Crowley, Roger. *Conquerors: How Portugal Forged the First Global Empire.* New York, NY: Random House, 2015.

Marsh, Carol. *Pedro Álvares Cabral: Discoverer of Brazil.* Peachtree City, GA: Gallopade International, 2004.

Mooney, Carla. *Explorers of the New World: Discover the Golden Age of Exploration with 22 Projects.* White River Junction, VT: Nomad Press, 2011.

Nicole, David. *The Portuguese in the Age of Discovery: c. 1340–1665.* Oxford, England: Osprey, 2012.

Roberts, Adrian. *The Age of Discovery.* Auckland, New Zealand: Horsham House, 2014.

Ross, Stewart. *Into the Unknown: How Great Explorers Found Their Way by Land, Sea, and Air.* Somerville, ME: Candlewick, 2011.

BIBLIOGRAPHY

Caminho, Pero Vaz. "Letter of Pero Vaz de Caminho." In *Portuguese Voyages 1498–1663*, ed. Charles David Lay. New York, NY: Dutton and Company. Retrieved December 18, 2015 (http://blogs .uoregon.edu/summerinstitute2013/files/2013/05 /The-Letter-of-Pero-Vaz-de-Caminha-21jx6cx.pdf).

Cavendish, Richard. "Cabral Discovers Brazil." *History Today*, Vol. 50, No. 4, April 2000. Retrieved November 16, 2015 (http://www.historytoday.com /richard-cavendish/cabral-discovers-brazil).

Explorers & Discoverers of the World. "Pedro Alvares Cabral." Gale, 1993. *Biography in Context.* Retrieved November 16, 2015 (http://ic.galegroup .com/).

MacClymont, James Roxburg, William Brooks Greenlee, and Pero Vaz de Caminho. *Pedro Cabral*. Ed. Keith Bridgeman and Tahira Arsham. England: Viartis, 2009.

Mariners' Museum. "Pedro Álvares Cabral." Retrieved November 16, 2015 (http://exploration .marinersmuseum.org/subject/pedro-alvares -cabral/).

Vaucher, Jean. "Development of Sailing Ships." Pages Historique, Université de Montréal Department of Information and Research, 2014. Retrieved December 29, 2015 (http://www.iro.umontreal .ca/~vaucher/History/Ships_Discovery/).

About the Author

Born in Newport News, Virginia, the home of the Mariners' Museum and not far from where early explorers came to North America, Ann Byers has always loved the sea and ships. As a child, she sometimes sat at the harbor, watching as ships came in, identifying their countries' flags. She enjoyed traveling to spots on the Atlantic where English, Spanish, and French adventurers landed. Now she lives on the other coast, in California, and visits the places where people from Russia, China, Japan, and Korea first came to America.

Byers is a descendant of one of the explorers who settled Jamestown, the first permanent colony in what is now the United States.

Photo Credits

Designer: Nicole Russo; Editor: Meredith Day; Photo Researcher: Karen Huang